skate
boarding

Design and creation: GRAPH'M

ISBN: 2-7528-0010-X
Publisher code: T00010

Copyright registration: October 2004
Printed in Singapore by Tien Wah Press

www.fitwaypublishing.com
Fitway Publishing
12, avenue d'Italie - 75627 Paris cedex 13

extreme Sports

skate
boarding

fabrice le mao
photographs mathias fennetaux

fitway.
publishing

contents

Sustainable development

A sport?

'Skateboarding, a sport? Rubbish, it's a fad! Like hula-hoops and yo-yos!' Every skateboarder has heard this remark at least once in their life. Since the early 1960s, few people have really taken skateboarding seriously. And there is a reason for this: most skateboarders are under twenty and they usually hang around in groups in the street. In fact, there is no doubt about it: skateboarders are an essential part of youth culture.

Non-skateboarders are often disconcerted by the sport. It is both fluid like surfing and spectacularly 'acrobatic' like snowboarding. Skateboarders explore urban space in a way that often surpasses the most imaginative ideas of urban designers. As Craig R. Stecyk III, one of the leading journalists on the sport, wrote: 'Two hundred years of American technology has unwittingly created a massive cement playground of unlimited potential. But it was the minds of eleven year olds that could see that potential.'

Mickael McKrodt, San Sebastian, 2004, Free session.

Surfing, the big brother?

It has been suggested that skateboarding was born out of the unlikely union of a joke and a challenge, the type of beginning that can produce the best or the worst offspring. The baby-boom of the late 1950s created an unprecedented demand for a variety of games and sports – all those children swarming around the suburbs of the big cities needed something to do. In the streets of Venice Beach and Santa Monica, California; on the concrete drives along the shores of Waikiki; on the island of Oahu, Hawaii; the kids dreamed of surfing and speed.

Who actually invented skateboarding? Who first had the idea to put together the ill-assorted parts consisting of a plank of wood measuring 5 x 10 cm (2 x 4 in) and the remains of dismantled skates? A surfer with no waves? A kid fed up with his scooter being like everyone else's? It could be either or both. The joke is that, of course, it was born by mistake. The challenge is that, ever since the four metal or clay wheels (which is what skate wheels were first made of) were placed on the ground, there has been a constant flow of ideas as to how such an object might be used.

In 1959, the first mass-produced boards came on to the market. At first, there were not enough to satisfy demand and the quality was mediocre. The manufacturers were

Left: *Consumer society paved the way for leisure society. The revival of surfing in the first half of the 20th century saw the beginning of activities focused on solitary sporting performance.*

Right: *Sidewalk Surf, Surf Skeeter, Roll'n Surf … The first skateboard brands were directly linked to the world of surfing. It was not until the early 1970s that its urban counterpart hit the headlines.*
Bob Garza private collection, fibre glass surfboard, California, 2002.

more interested in profit than in research and development and poor design; in particular, the clay wheels, which had little grip, led to a wave of accidents and even a few fatalities. Skateboarding became labelled as dangerous, cities banned the practice and parents stopped buying the boards.

Surfers, however, were not deterred. What better antidote to a lack of waves? On their half-metre 'surf-skeeters' they perfected their turns and style. Almost all early skateboards were home-made, which explains why the first boards were shaped like surfboards. In the early 1960s, every self-respecting surfer had a skateboard. It is no coincidence that Hobie, the famous brand associated with surfing, was also one of the market leaders of skateboards until the early 1970s.

Left: *As soon as it appeared in the late 1950s, skateboarding became a favourite subject for photographers. What can surpass photographs that mix sport and the urban environment?*

Right: *The almost religious fascination of the skater with his equipment: for him, it has a soul of its own.*

From the **stone** age
to the **titanium era**

Some people say that skateboarding was born in 1959 because this is when boards first became commercially available, but many do not agree that this is its official birthday. Before this date, skateboards were made in garages and workshops; of solid wood which gave almost no non-slip surface, the truck (the device that holds the wheels) was minuscule and barely adjustable, and the wheels were made of metal or clay with hardly any bearings, so that they had absolutely no grip or inertia. These early skateboards were often lethal contraptions.

It was not until the first half of the 1960s that skateboarding revealed its real potential. Frank Nasworthy, an engineer who was fanatical about aeronautics and surfing, had the brilliant idea of using urethane to make skateboard wheels. This is a type of plastic developed during World War II which was being used to make roller skate wheels in the 1960s. The result was amazing: urethane reduces vibrations and can be made to varying degrees of hardness, so altering and improving the grip on the ground.

By the late 1960s, skateboard design had come a long way. The board was invariably made of glued laminated timber, since fibre glass and metal had been tried but were considered to be too dangerous. Some truck manufacturers added springs and varying angles for the axis which gave added manoeuvrability but skaters often preferred the simplicity of the original design. As for the wheels, since the advent of urethane, they now come in every colour and shape.

Opposite : *A stack of skateboards. On tour, a skateboard may only last for one trick and will rarely last more than two or three days.*

Above: *Chad Muska posing for a shot, or perhaps thinking about his forthcoming album with the biggest American rappers, or maybe thinking about a design for a new style of shoe. But then again, he may be simply enjoying skating with some music in the background.*

During the 1970s, skateboards became wider and precision bearing wheels increased traction and so allowed increased speed. The 1980s and 1990s brought further small revolutions in materials but the glued laminated timber board has remained a great classic. Titanium occasionally, and expensively, replaces aluminium and wheels become more complex with the emergence of hollow cores, but the fascination that goes with every stage of buying a board is at least as intense as when skateboarders made their own.

The development of equipment followed and, at the same time, fostered the growth of skating tricks. The urban environment offers a physical challenge limited only by the imagination.

Battling with the urban jungle

Sealed bearings and ease of adjustment meant that by the mid-1970s, the technology was in place and all there was to do was to go out and do battle with the skating sites. Having been born in the streets and alleys of the suburbs, skateboarding gradually evolved into a craze that exploited the possibilities of car parks, school playgrounds, empty swimming pools and reservoirs, as well as the large urban spaces created by modern architecture. The aim of the skateboarders was to achieve the weightlessness and speed of the surfer riding a wave.

Paradoxically, it was this desire to follow closely in the footsteps of its predecessor, surfing, that finally caused the two sports to break away from each other. The urban landscape is so rich that, very quickly, new architectural developments give rise to new ideas for skating and, as the skateboarder gains in skill, so fresh challenges are sought. To be a skateboarder, you need to be able to adapt to your environment, take every opportunity as if there were no tomorrow and leave no remorse or regrets behind. One surprising thing about skateboarding, compared to other boardsports, is that it gives teenage kids the opportunity to gain control over the environment where they previously had none. Suddenly, with the help of a home-made object the urban landscape is reinvented for no purpose other than the thrill of enjoying it.

This revolution of the urban environment began in California, between Venice Beach and Santa Monica, alongside the shell of a former amusement park

Opposite and following double page: *Skating at night quickly became attractive and exciting. At night, the urban landscape is rid of its irritating killjoys: pedestrians and cars. The urban jungle is there for the taking!*

nicknamed Dogtown. A shop named Zephyr Surf & Skate Shop put together a team of skateboarders made up of kids from the area. The kids were keen to be in the surfing team, but it was skateboarding which would propel them to the heights of fame. They were called the Z Boys because of the name of the shop, but were nicknamed the Dogtowners because of their attitude on and off their skateboards: they were 'dogs' in a 'dogtown'. To begin with, the competitions took place in a good-natured atmosphere but the Dogtowners changed all that. They were street kids, often from broken families, and they skated with the determination of the underdog. Skateboarding was no longer an innocent game or a sport for frustrated skiers or surfers. A lifestyle was born.

Skateparks were born in the early 1970s in response to urgent needs: skaters needed to create skatable 'waves' and the public authorities needed to limit the risk of accidents. This is the skatepark in Marseilles, created in the mid 1980s, and considered to be one of the ten best in the world.

Somewhat ironically, handrails, which were designed to prevent accidents associated with the use of steps, became a source of danger for skaters who needed to measure the accuracy of their movements with great precision to avoid falling.

'Skate and destroy!'

In January 1981, a new magazine appeared across the United States, its name, *Thrasher*, evoking and encompassing everything that a real skateboarder should be in the urban jungle. The magazine was produced by a small organisation based in San Francisco, and it quickly overshadowed everything that had previously been published in the genre. Going against the grain of the time, the editorial team wrote copy that was anything but smooth and bland, giving the world of skateboarding an urban feel, with urban values of uncompromising toughness and a hint of latent violence. Dedicated skateparks, which had been built by the hundred in the 1970s, gradually disappeared due to prohibitively high insurance premiums and the rise in the cost of land. In any case, skateparks that skateboarders had to pay for were by no means necessary. Why should anyone pay for an hour of skateboarding in a policed environment when the streets offered vast possibilities entirely free of charge and authority? In the eyes of a skateboarder, the city has no limits, and modern architecture with its walkways, ramps, tunnels and walls offers endless opportunities for tricks.

Opposite and following double page:
How do you define creativity? Hijacking urban street furniture and using it in ways far from its primary function is one answer. Every situation is a pretext for new ideas for skaters.

Most skateboarders master their sport without stadiums, tracks or training rooms. Nevertheless, the concentration and perseverance needed to master this heel flip 180 is the same as that needed to get to the top in any other sport.

No one has sat on this bench for a long time. It is opposite the station in Barcelona and is too exposed to the sun and the noise of the city. Here it is given a new lease of life.

Based on the idea of challenging the urban landscape, *Thrasher* launched a slogan: 'Skate and destroy' which quickly caught on, becoming part of the collective consciousness of the readers. The anarchist tone was intended to incite skateboarders to push against their own limits in an increasingly demanding urban world. Street skateboarding provided millions of teenagers with a means of expression that combined sport and creativity and this was unheard of in the sporting world. Once again, skateboarding spread like lightning through the city streets of the world. Pavements; business centres; shopping centres; activity centres; industrial estates; anything with tarmac or cement was explored. The most insignificant objects in the urban landscape were redefined and acquired a use that had not been apparent when they were designed, to the great displeasure of city dwellers. Even in Moscow, communism had a hard time resisting the free spirit of skateboarders.

Thrasher became the skateboarder's bible and soon invented a new slogan: 'Skate and create' meaning: 'If you don't find what you like in the city, build your own ideal environment'. The effect was astounding: a plethora of ramps and mini-ramps appeared in gardens, garages, disused warehouses and anywhere else where a 'skatable' could be built undisturbed. The wood used was recycled, borrowed or bought by any means necessary, it did not matter. Suddenly there was a generation of instant constructors of equipment. This was unheard of in the sporting world: sportspeople creating their own structures! Less laudable was the bad press which skateboarding received as complaints increased of menacing 'pavement vandals'.

In the mid 1980s, Natas Kaupas did the impossible until then by using a single movement to take him from a horizontal surface (the ground) to a vertical surface (a wall). This night shot demonstrates the beauty of the move.

The **ups** and the **downs**

Is the history of skateboarding a series of fads or a series of slow moves towards acceptance? It is generally agreed that there have been four successive waves of interest in skateboarding.

At the very beginning, it was a hobby for kids left to their own devices. Its hybrid and simple nature, neither roller skating nor surfing, stopped it being taken seriously. Pop groups such as the Beach Boys wrote songs such as *Surfin' USA* and *Sidewalk Surfin'*, and fashion models posed on skateboards for magazine covers. The famous *Life* magazine even featured a photograph of a girl doing a headstand on a board, but the first wave of popularity hardly spread beyond the United States, a country always willing to embrace new fashions and activities. Fears about safety peaked in the mid-1960s, bringing the first wave of interest to an end.

Left: *The magazine that always foresees the latest trends, Life, put skateboarding on the front page in 1963. That appearance was all that was needed to send 'Sidewalk Surfing' rocketing to fame.*

Right: *Despite the magazine front pages, the adverts and the profusion of celebrities using the skateboard image to sell themselves to the media, skating remained an activity that took place largely away from the public eye.*

The second wave took it further. The progress of technology opened up unseen possibilities and both the boards and the sport moved faster and more easily. Manoeuvres and gymnastic tricks based on surfing formed the bedrock of skateboarding skills until skateboarders, using empty swimming pools, developed a range of new skills using the curved sides of the pools as banking. It was fortunate for skateboarding that the great drought of the 1970s banned pool owners from filling their pools! Skateboarding merged with popular culture as skateboarders embraced the rebel spirit of rock'n'roll, and then, towards the end of the 1970s, of the emerging punk rock movement. However, escalating insurance premiums forced many skateparks to close and by the end of 1980, skateboarding was entering another slump.

Opposite and following double page: *A colourful replica of a Californian pool in the Spanish Basque country, a few sponsors, some skaters, that is all you need to produce an exciting contest.*

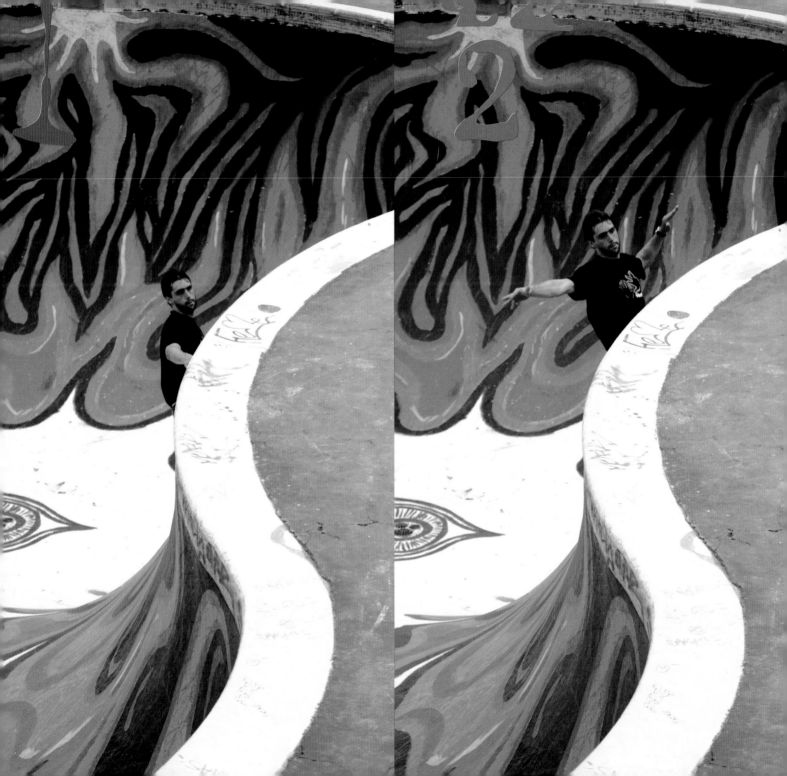

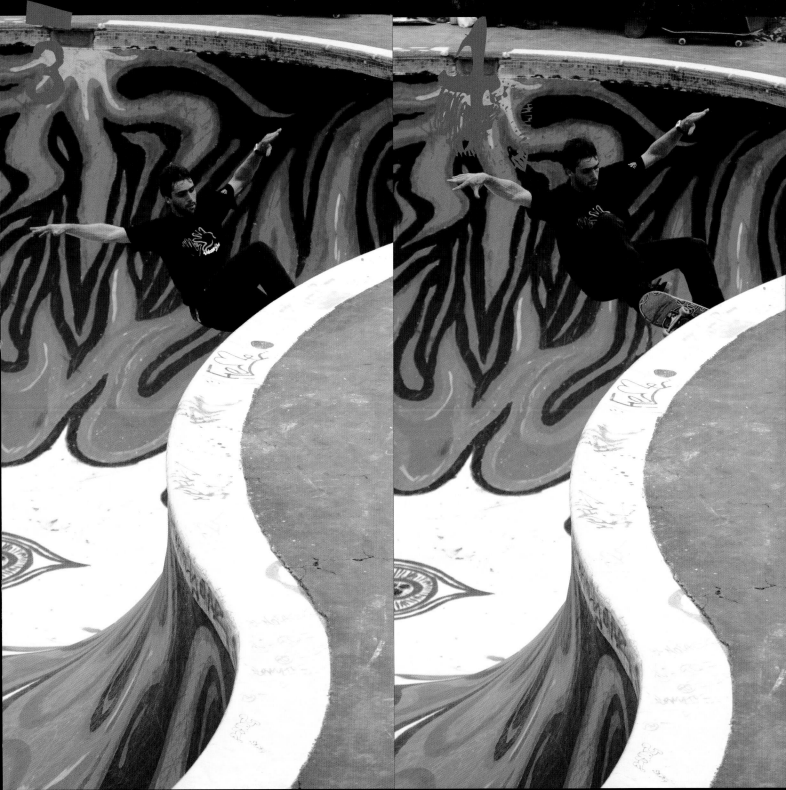

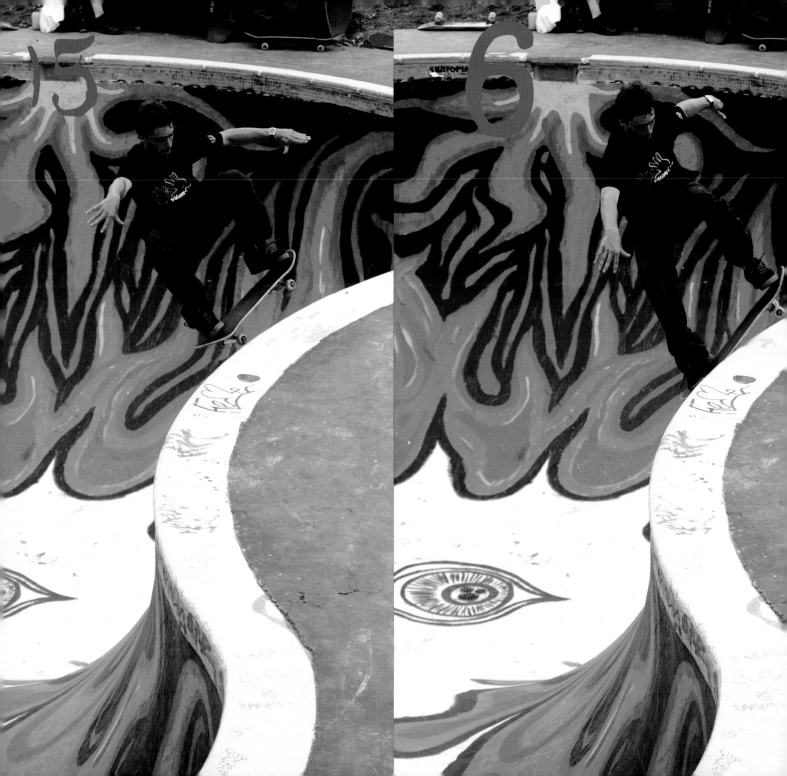

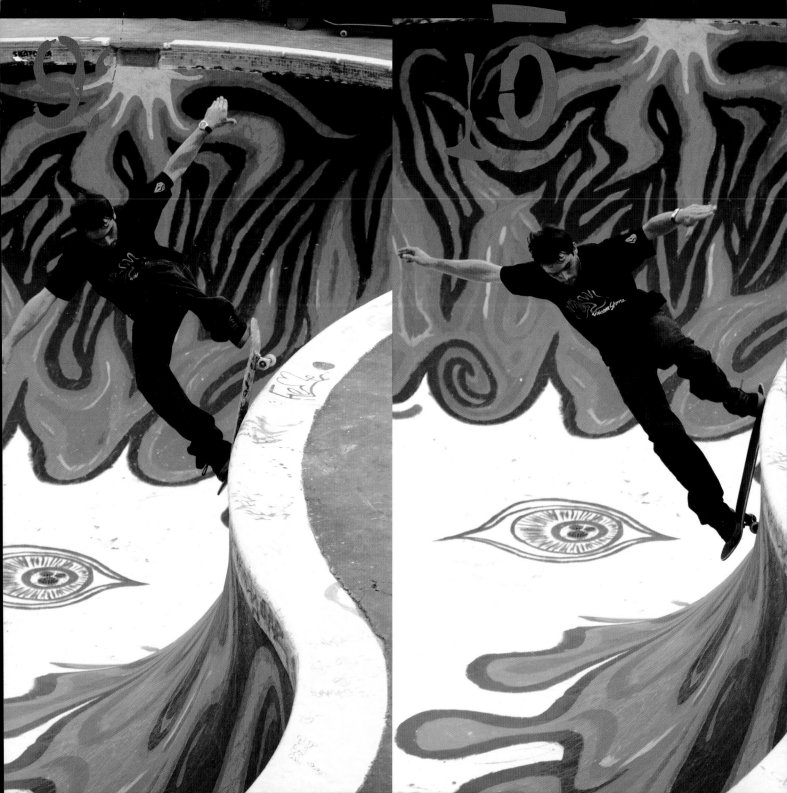

It was a return to the streets that was to underpin the revival of skateboarding during the 1980s, combined with the emergence of 'vert' or vertical skateboarding on home-made wooden skate ramps. A new set of champion skateboarders burst on the scene, made up of youngsters who turned professional although they were still at school. These kids earned royalties that were higher than the salaries of their teachers and parents. Stars like Tony Hawk, Steve Caballero, Matt Hensley, Mark Gonzales, Natas Kaupas and a whole host of other pros were propelled into a level of professionalism that was new to skateboarding. A world tournament and worldwide media coverage enabled skateboarding to discover a whole new audience. It even became part of the Olympic Games though only as a demonstration sport. The public reaction to skateboarding varied from one continent to another and from one country to another, but on the whole, it was still perceived as a problem by the general public. At best, skateboards were viewed as toys and skateboarders as slightly backward teenagers whose activity was an outcome of the growth of a leisure society. At worst, they were seen as a nuisance and juvenile delinquents out to damage public property.

Nevertheless, the creative aspect of the sport grew in importance, especially in the eyes of the advertisers and media who were well aware of the visual and innovative appeal. For skateboarders in the 1990s, despite another slump in interest in the middle of the decade, doors and minds began to open. Styles remained varied; you could be into street skating or keen on using ramps and skateparks. As the stars became more charismatic and more open to appealing to the media, Tony Hawk became an international symbol by agreeing to be the hero in a video game that sold several million copies. The first Extreme Games in Rhode Island in 1995 brought a great deal of exposure and also an influx of advertisers keen to use skateboarding for promotional purposes. Something else was new; skateboarding had lasted a generation, it had earned its place in the minds and affections of millions of people across the world.

Covered wooden skateparks appeared in the early 1990s. They were a real training boon for skaters and enabled millions of them – who did not have the benefit of the Californian climate – to make progress undisturbed. This led to the emergence of many European talents on the world scene.

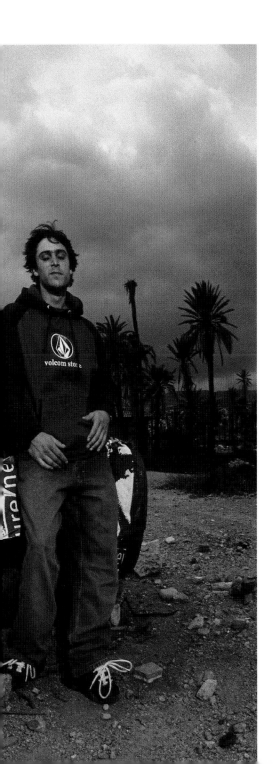

Skateboarding is **different**

No coach, no timetable, no location or equipment restrictions, no hierarchy, a natural respect for those who are better than you – these features, which are at the heart of skateboarding, are also the reason why the activity is not immediately defined as a sport by the person in the street. But then, skateboarding is, quite simply, not like other sports – 90 per cent of skateboarding is done in the street and 75 per cent of skateboarders are under twenty. There are estimated to be sixteen million skateboarders in the world and they would doubtless agree that skateboarding is not simply a sport, it is a lifestyle. Skateboarding intersects with music, film, fashion and art on the one hand and surfing, snowboarding, roller skating and BMX on the other, demonstrating that we are dealing with something more inspiring than a simple sporting activity. What sport, apart from the martial arts, can boast that it reaches beyond the scope of simply doing it?

However, it can be hard for the person in the street to appreciate what skateboarding really consists of. A teenager skateboards along for a few metres, then jumps in the air. The board turns and the skateboarder lands on it. Then the skater is on the pavement, or leaping into the road, apparently playing games with pedestrians and cars. It's more natural to accuse a skater of damaging the handrail of a staircase or a marble ledge in a public square than to see the skill involved in skating down a handrail. The skateboarder is likely to be dismissed as a boisterous, contemptuous teenager who does not care about other people, therefore the impression of being different is very real. Skateboarders may be seen as intruders or aliens in the city, but they are the people who are at the forefront of redefining the notion of what is urban. Moreover, they make good use of those undefined urban spaces which are otherwise the haunt of junkies, dealers and vagrants.

Generating **trends**

When Tony Alva launched his own brand of boards in 1979, not only was he one of the first pro skateboarders to turn his passion into a business, but he did so with an unprecedented approach to marketing and advertising. This desire to be different inspired innovative developments. When you spend a large proportion of your time and energy perfecting your style and technique and controlling your body in space, logic dictates that you will have a particular interest in art. Without wishing to portray all skateboarders as closet artists, the fact is that there are many examples that speak for themselves.

Spike Jonze, who was born Adam Spiegel, is known the world over for his famous film *Being John Malkovich*, which came out in 1999, and more recently for another film, *Adaptation*, but it was through photographing skaters and making skateboarding videos that he learned to work with composition and light. Through his camera lens, Jason Lee often improvised characters between two sequences. Jason has since gone into a full-time acting career. His supporting roles (*Dogma, Almost Famous, American Cuisine, Kissing A Fool, Enemy of the State, Heartbreakers,* etc.) are sometimes more powerful and lifelike than some of his leading roles. Steve Berra has not yet made the front page of the film magazines, but Guy Ritchie, also known as Mr Madonna, and the director of *Snatch,* is working on directing one of his scripts.

On the small screen, the members of the Jackass gang, stars of the eponymous MTV series, almost all came from the magazine, *Big Brother,* the skateboarding equivalent of the martial arts magazine, *Hara-Kiri.*

Opposite and right: *A blank wall becomes a huge canvas and a slope a means of redefining your balance. It is all a question of angles, when you think about it. The ability to see city streets in a different way often enables skaters to also imagine their lives and their relationships in a new way.*

The stunts and gags of mainstream skateboarding might now be viewed as absurdly technical but they were almost all conceived from the 'what if?' attitudes which prevail during skateboarding sessions.

Just as surprisingly, the skateboarding artists, Ed Templeton and Mark Gonzales, who have very different styles, are captivating the world of contemporary art. Ed Templeton has exhibited in Paris, in the prestigious Palais de Tokyo, while Mark continues with his exhibitions and 'performances' in Germany, Italy, Paris and New York.

Craig Stecyk and Glen E. Friedman were the first, in the mid 1970s, to build bridges between the worlds of skateboarding and artistic creation. Glen was starting out as a photographer, while Stecyk already had experience as a journalist. They both captured the essence of the Dogtown era of the 1970s. Very early on, Stecyk invented advertising and designs that reinforced the notion of an alternative boardsports culture. In the same period, Friedman became increasingly proficient as a photographer working with punk/hardcore pop bands such as Public Enemy, Run DMC, the Beastie Boys, Fugazi, Henry Rollins and LLCool J. Stecyk and Friedman were art director and co-producer for the documentary film, *Dogtown and Z boys* (2002), which won two awards at the Sundance Festival and was directed by Stacy Peralta, a former pro and joint owner of the famous brand, Powell Peralta. Stecyk is also the organiser of *Surf Culture* at the Laguna Art Museum in California. This the first art exhibition to consider the development of surfing as a cultural activity and to document the way in which art and surfing have cross-fertilised each other.

All skateboarders, whether professional or not, have an influence on the art world because of the way in which the activity links different social and cultural worlds – skateboarding is an inspiring image and is full of innovative activity in its own right. It seems hardly surprising that some artists deeply appreciate the creativity that comes from the sport.

Opposite and following double page: *Skateboarding offers the photographer an almost unlimited number of possibilities. Urban architecture and natural or artificial light open the way for an intensity of interest that endures over time.*

MEAT IS
MURDE

Many skaters are vegetarian. Without wishing to imply that the subject of this stroboscope also wrote the graffiti 'meat is murder', there is a good chance that he agrees with the slogan.

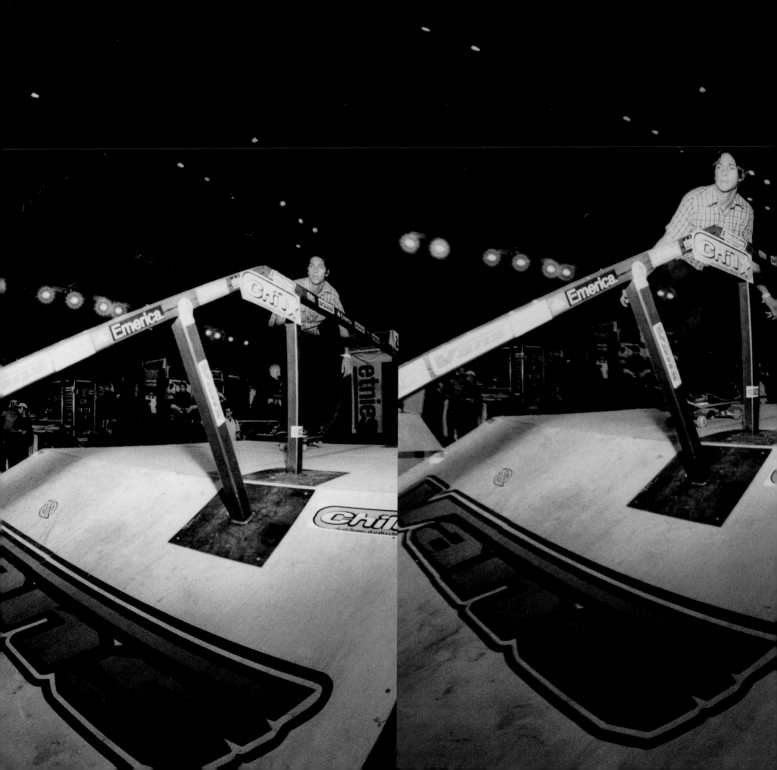

**Previous double
page and opposite:**
*Heath Kirchart does
not generally like
competitions.
His motivation has
more to do with the fact
that they give him the
opportunity to travel or
to see friends whom he
would not see otherwise.
In competitions,
the winner may appear to
be the skater who comes
first but the 'real' winner
might be the one who has
the most fun.*

The **competitive spirit** without **competition**

The concept of competition, with its barrage of rules, large number of competitors and quest for glory that it too often generates has never really been taken up in the history of skateboarding. In 1975, the Bahne Cadillac International, in Del Mar, California, was one of the first competitions to offer a serious interface between the public and those doing the sport. Slalom and freestyle were the two disciplines of the weekend. Although there was every reason to expect a standard competition, the eleven skateboarders were determined to prove that the judging system did not hold water by demonstrating an entirely new way of skateboarding. A constant movement towards revolution is the only lasting tradition in the history of the competition.

In the 1980s, this meant going all out to find competition formats and sites that were interesting both for skateboarders and for spectators. The longest slide, the highest aerial, the jam session, solo or duo elimination, man on man – they tried everything, but what always emerged as the real motivation was the pleasure of meeting, having a good time together and assessing your own progress compared with that of others. Of course, results counted for the sponsors, who could make or break careers depending on rankings, but as a general rule, a good, charismatic skateboarder who was idolised and respected by the kids was more important than a fierce competitor.

Whether they like skating alone or in a group, skaters are always seeking the satisfaction of the perfect move. Their taste is for personal excellence rather than for victory.

Sustainable development

Whether they were hosted for the general public or held totally underground, often the sole pretext for competitions was to enable people to meet up. Styles became so distinct from one person to the next that, at the end of the 1980s, judging was more a subjective affair than a genuine analysis of the tricks done by each competitor. Why should trick X get a better mark than figure Y?

Media coverage raised the level of interest in skateboarding as a spectator sport in the early 1990s, especially after ESPNs first Extreme Games at Rhode Island in 1995. However, shortly after this, the video boom relegated media coverage of competitions to secondary importance only. Competitors asked themselves why they should risk injury at a competition where the media coverage was uncertain, when making a good video could generate marketing for months? This simple calculation meant that skateboarding soon lost the attention of the mass media again. Since then, stars such as Eric Koston and Mike Carroll have tried to take advantage of the presence of journalists at competitions to make their performance a statement. Koston, for example, takes a wicked pleasure from spicing up his runs with tricks, mixing comedy and technique.

Ramp skating is more spectacular and therefore more media-friendly than street skating, especially when it is done in front of a landscape like this. The tricks developed on the ramp sometimes appear on the front page of the international media, this being the case with Tony Hawk's famous 900, which made headline news on all the American TV bulletins.

Made by **skateboarders** for **skateboarders**

The skateboarding market came a long way from the home-made stage in the early 1960s to being worth millions of dollars in the 1990s. From the late 1970s, equipment production (boards, wheels and trucks) was controlled by a handful of businessmen. In the majority of cases, they were engineers fresh out of university or surfers who already owned board factories, who wanted to gain additional income from this lucrative market. For nearly thirty years, the system worked perfectly well. The big companies generated enough capital to create research and development departments in their companies, compensating for their lack of adaptability towards better product quality.

In the mid 1980s, the skateboard business was shared between four big brands: Powell-Peralta; Vision/Sims; Santa Cruz/SMA; and H-Street/Planet Earth. When the market began to become saturated, the professionals wanted to change things and a handful of them decided to take their destiny into their own hands. Steve Rocco was one of the first to launch his own brand: Santa Monica Airlines Rocco Division, which became World Industries after a few weeks. Its marketing campaigns did not hesitate to mock the big names. It was an immediate success, the kids loved the brand and identified with it.

One board with trucks and four wheels: the business of skating appears simple. In reality however, it is much more complex. Authenticity is of prime value.

In the two years that followed, a plethora of professionals followed Rocco's example with varying degrees of success. Out of this welter of small brands, some were badly distributed, badly run and born out of impulse, but enough of them succeeded to create a major change: the big brands were soon overtaken by their smaller rivals. In a bittersweet environment, the 1990s levelled off the market. In order to survive, the big brands were forced to restructure. They abandoned their hierarchical structure in favour of increased customer communication. Those who could not, did not survive.

At the same time, the formerly small brands restructured themselves but, unlike their forerunners in previous decades, they kept in mind the prime objective: to serve the cause of skateboarding. 'By skaters, for skaters' was their maxim. The mistrust of anything that does not come from within skateboarding circles is very real. This creates a link between skateboarders and the market for skateboarding goods.

Many multi-nationals have come a cropper in the skate business. The skaters might seem inoffensive at first glance but they are sometimes tougher than sponsors think. This is the lighthouse in Biarritz, in front of La Chambre d'Amour, a top surfing beach.

Towards **recognition**

Public recognition is not something that skateboarders have pursued. Traditionally, they mock fame until it knocks on their door. Tony Hawk, the eighth most famous sports personality among teenagers according to sport magazine polls across the world, knows a lot about this. An unrivalled skater since the early 1980s, he won many competitions and invented numerous tricks, but worldwide fame came only after the production of the video game, *Pro Skater* which sold several million copies worldwide. Fame then snowballed and he appeared on television, in commercials, at media events, and he now presents a programme on MTV.

However, recognition is not necessarily the same thing as fame. The latter is often short-lived, while the former is won over the long term by hard work and consistency.

The strength of a sport often lies in its capacity to capture the interest of the presenters as well as the spectators. While skateboarding is visually rich, for most people it has great difficulty getting past the curiosity stage. It is not a sport for those primarily interested in team or combat sports. Instead, it attracts those interested in self control, strong concentration, bravery, physical skill, adaptability and originality. It is not always easy to appreciate the skills

Half rock star, half sporting rebel; professional skaters live for their passion. Their careers and professional lives mostly take place in the street. What could be easier than adapting the show for an audience that is always demanding more new things?

involved in skateboarding; performing a trick with apparent ease does not mean that there is no physical tension or concentration.

Commercial sponsorship and interest by the general public remain problems for the viability of the sport. If skateboarding does not interest major sports companies and consumers, it has no chance of touching hearts. Nike, McDonalds and Coca-Cola have all used skateboarding images in adverts, but have been slow to invest in the sporting side of it until recently.

Intrinsically, skateboarding has never been a popular sport in the usual sense of the word: reasonably accessible to whoever wishes to do it. It is one of those sports for individuals who like taking risks. It is a sport which has endured and which is showing a new buoyancy; it can be enjoyed at any level, and especially by those kids immersed in an urban environment and in youth street culture. Where will it go? It is already enjoyed by the sixteen million people who skateboard all over the world, and its forthcoming entry into the Olympic Games (it was already a demonstration sport at the Sydney Olympic Games in 2000) opens the gates wide for the future.

'You were born in the gutter and to the gutter you will return'. This could be the skater's eleventh commandment. But how great to taste success when you started from the street!

The power of television in particular

and the media in general is that it makes possible great visibility. With time (it has been in existence for forty years!) skateboarding has gradually lost its image of being merely a game. But if it is not a game, neither can it be called art, despite the fact that many creative people (designers, painters, sculptors, photographer and film directors) have incorporated it into their work. Is it a sport? The answer is probably yes, but an unacknowledged one. Sporting magazines do not often feature it, but perhaps that doesn't matter because, for skateboarders, results are not as important as simply getting on a board and skating.

From the lone kid skating along a pavement on his board to the heroes of modern skateboarding like Danny Way, Eric Koston and Tony Hawk, the possibilities are immense, and it is up to each kid who takes up skateboarding to discover all the subtleties.

This trick is called a frontside smith grind. It is one of the basic skate tricks in which style is of great importance. 'Style is everything' is one of the sacred laws of skating that no one ever mentions but which you must learn if you are to succeed as a skater.

180: measurement of rotation in degrees, often combined with a qualifier defining the trick.

360: see 180.

5-0: grind with only the rear truck.

50/50: grind with trucks.

900: two and a half revolutions. Tony Hawk is the only person to have done this trick, in 1999.

A: followed by a value between 78 and 101: the hardness of a wheel.

Acid drop: trick invented by Duane Peters, which consists riding straight off something and freefalling to the ground.

Aerial: trick involving leaving a ramp or bowl holding the board with the hand(s) and coming back on to the curve.

Backside: having the back to the action.

Bar: metal bar.

Bank: incline.

Baseplate: part of the truck screwed to the board.

Bigspin: 360 combined with a 180 of the body in the opposite direction.

Blindside: trick in which the field of visibility is nil.

Blunt: being on an object with the wheels on top of it and the tail pressed against the vertical part of the object.

Board: the whole board, or just the deck.

Boned: trick in which the leg is stretched out straight; style and difficulty points guaranteed.

Boneless: putting the foot in front on the ground, catching the board with the hand and jumping back on the board.

Cab: short for Steve Caballero, the inventor of the fakie 360 on the ramp.

Casper: trick in which the board is turned over with the wheels facing skyward, one foot on it (back foot on the tail), the other underneath. Balancing on the back foot. A freestyle trick common in street skating.

Caveman: any trick done 'old style'.

Concave: lengthways curved edges of the board.

Coping: rounded edge on the top of ramps, pools and other skatable modules, of metal, PVC or concrete.

Coper: piece of PVC added to trucks for easier grinds or to prevent wear on coping and/or truck.

Curb: pavement or edge of pavement, but also any urban object that is similar to it.

Deck: board.

Disaster: having done a 180 in the air, the skater is balanced on the coping or handrail.

Downhill: discipline of pure speed.

Drop in: entering a ramp, starting from the coping.

Emb:

(short for 'Embarcadero')

a legendary San Diego skating location in the 1990s.

Fakie: skating backwards.

Feeble: grind where only the rear truck sits on the module.

Flat: any trick (flat trick) done on the ground.

Flip: complete rotation of the board round its longitudinal axis.

Focus: breaking the board in two pieces (minimum) on purpose, out of frustration.

Freestyle: discipline involving only flat tricks. In competition, freestylers do routines choreographed to music of their choice.

Frontside: facing forwards during the action.

Funbox: platform with various inclines in a skatepark.

Goofy: someone who skates with the right foot in front.

Grab: grabbing the board during a trick.

Grind: trick consisting of grinding the truck on a surface like a handrail. The combined feelings of balance and friction are unparalleled in the world of sport.

Griptape: a grip stuck to the board.

Halfcab: fakie 180 (half a Cab)

Half-pipe: half of a pipeline. Until the 1980s, half-pipes had no flat surface between the two curves.

Handplant: ramp trick involving balancing on one arm at the top of the ramp, like a handstand.

Hanger: the upper part of the truck.

Hangup: catching the rear truck on the top of the module, often resulting in a fall.

Impossible: flat trick in which the board does a complete rotation around the back foot while the skater jumps in the air.

Indy grab: backside aerial with the rear hand grabbing the board.

Jam: competition format in which all competitors skate one after the other, however they like.

Kink: defect on the ramp or module.

Glossary

Lip: edge of a module, whether or not it is built for skating.

Lipslide: sliding along the lip.

Manual: skating balanced on the back or front wheels.

Mctwist: 540 degree rotation in the air on a ramp with the head down. Invented by Mike McGill.

Mini-ramp: small ramp, more fun and accessible than the normal ramp.

Nollie: ollie done in reverse with the nose.

Nose: the nose of the board.

Ollie: trick consisting of smacking the tail on the ground and jumping in the air with the board. The feet do a scissors movement, holding the board to the soles of the feet. Invented by Alan 'Ollie' Gelfand in the late seventies.

Park or skatepark: an area built for skateboarding.

Pro: short for professional; any person who makes a living from skating.

Quarter-pipe: a street module.

Regular: someone who skates with the left foot in front.

Revert: finishing a trick by pushing the wheels backwards so that they skid 180 degrees and go into a fakie.

Rock'n'roll: trick consisting of balancing the middle of the board on a ramp or handrail, before turning 180 degrees to move off. Called boardslide in street skating.

Slalom: similar to the skiing discipline.

Slappy: grinding a curb without using an ollie.

Slick: plastic material stuck on to some boards to extend their lifespan and make them slide better.

Smith grind: trick that involves grinding with the rear truck and the edge of the board on the curb or coping, while the front wheels are not touching anything.

Snake: a long and sinuous mini-ramp.

Snake: a situation when skaters drop on to the ramp in complete anarchy.

Spine: two ramps placed back to back.

Switch: skating the 'wrong' way around (a goofy like a regular and a regular like a goofy).

Tail: part of the board behind the rear truck.

Tailgrab: grabbing the tail of the board during a trick.

Tail slide: sliding on the tail of the board.

Transition: the rounded part of pools, quarter-pipes, half-pipes or full-pipes.

Truck: the metal part of the board. Originally a French invention.

Vert: the vertical part of a ramp or pool, and by extension, the ramp, as a discipline.

Wallie: ollie done from a wall.

Wallride: skating on a wall with or without the help of a module.

Wax: surfer's paraffin wax, used to make any urban furniture more conducive to skating tricks.

Further information

Books and magazines

Books

Brooke, Michael: ***The Concrete Wave: The History of Skateboarding,***
Warwick Publishing, 1999

Noll, Rhyn: ***Skateboard Retrospective,***
Schiffer Books, 2000

Magazines

Thrasher
High Speed Production, 1303 Underwood Ave., San Francisco, CA 94124, USA

Transworld Skateboarding
353 Airport Road, Oceanside, CA 92054, USA

Slap
High Speed Production, 1303 Underwood Ave., San Francisco, CA 94124, USA

Skateboarder
Primedia, Dana Point, CA 92629, USA

Juice
52 Market St., Venice, CA 90291, USA

Films and videos

Skateboard Madness, by Hal Jepsen **(1980)**

Thrashin', by David Winters **(1986)**

Police Academy 4, by Jim Drake **(1987)**

Gleaming the Cube, by Graeme Clifford **(1989)**

Dogtown and Z Boys, by Stacy Peralta **(2001)**

Grind, by Casey La Scala **(2003)**

Internet

www.fntofoto.com

www.slapmagazine.com

www.skateboarding.com

www.thrashermagazine.com

www.v7distribution.com

www.tumyeto.com

www.dlxsf.com

www.esfootwear.com